You
Might Be A
United
Methodist
If...

You Might Be A United Methodist If...

Robert Martin Walker

Book Design: Carol Williams

10 9 8 7 6 5 4 3 2 1   98 99 00 01 02 03

Library of Congress Cataloging-in-Publication Data

Walker, Robert Martin.
    You might be a United Methodist if— / Robert Martin Walker.
      p. cm.
    ISBN 0-8272-4407-X
    1. United Methodist Church (U.S.) —Membership—Humor.
  2. Methodist Church —United States—Membership—Humor. I. Title.
BX8331.2.W35   1998
287'.6' 0207—dc21
                                                              97-39362
                                                                    CIP

Introduction

When I think about United Methodism, a comment by a United States Supreme Court justice reflecting on pornography comes to mind: "I can't define it, but I know it when I see it."

United Methodism defies easy definition, as several General Conferences have discovered. The fact that most of us have trouble explaining United Methodism to outsiders isn't really a hindrance. We Methodists know who we are.

One thing I've always appreciated about Methodists is our ability to laugh at ourselves. And there's plenty in Methodism to chuckle over. I'm certain that I've only scratched the surface of United Methodist follies and peculiarities in this small book.

This volume of insider humor is offered in a spirit of goodwill and good faith. My intention is not to offend but to inspire...laughter and even some self-reflection. In laughter, we often discover the truth about ourselves.

So read and enjoy. If we pay attention to what we find funny about United Methodism, we will more clearly understand who we truly are—as United Methodists and as God's people.

Robert Martin Walker

You Might Be A United Methodist If...

you don't take a Rolaids
when your heart is strangely
warmed.

You Might Be A United Methodist If...

you know that
a "circuit rider"
is not an electrical device.

You **Might Be A** United **Methodist** If...

you think "UMW" stands for United Methodist Women rather than the United Mine Workers.

You Might Be A United Methodist If...

you realize that
the Book of Discipline is not
a guide to getting
your child to behave.

You Might Be A United Methodist If...

you felt that the NCAA penalties against SMU football were too harsh.

You Might Be A United Methodist If...

you've ever owned a pair of cross and flame boxer shorts.

You Might Be A United Methodist If...

you know that the Wesleyan Quadrilateral isn't a trick football play involving four lateral passes.

You Might Be A United Methodist If...

you have an unexplained yearning to visit Wesley's Chapel in London.

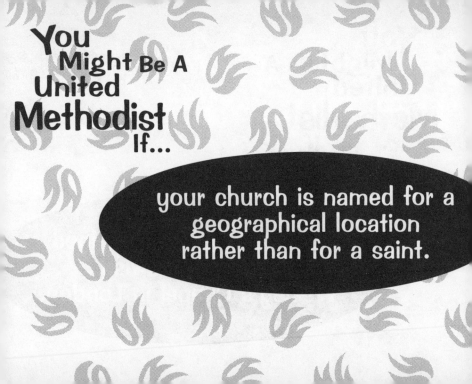

You Might Be A United Methodist If...

you've never heard a sermon on Hell and don't feel that you're missing out.

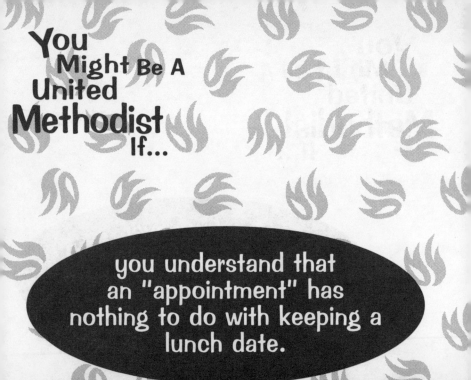

You Might Be A United Methodist If...

there's at least one person in every church meeting who says, "But we've never done it that way before."

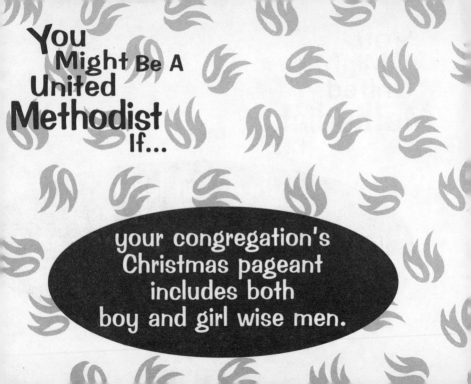

You Might Be A United Methodist If...

you accept
the fact that the hymn
"O, for a thousand tongues
to sing" has almost as many
stanzas as tongues.

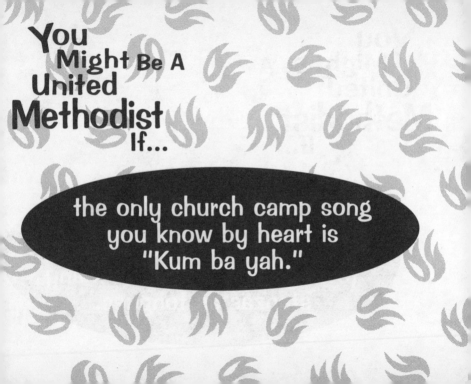

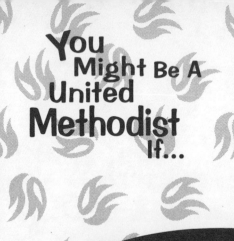

You Might Be A United Methodist If...

half the people sitting in your pew lip-sync the words to the hymns.

You Might Be A United Methodist If...

you consider the monthly potluck supper a sacrament.

You Might Be A United Methodist If...

you realize that VBS isn't a sexually transmitted disease.

You Might Be A United Methodist If...

"Good morning" has the status of a liturgical greeting in the worship service.

You Might Be A United Methodist If...

you sit while singing
"Stand up, stand up for Jesus."

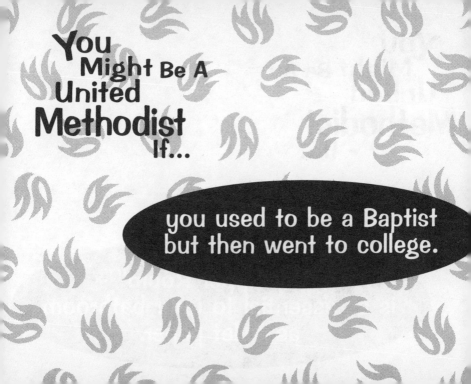

You Might Be A United Methodist If...

"The Upper Room" is as essential to your bathroom as toilet paper.

You Might Be A United Methodist If...

you realize that "potluck" doesn't refer to a random method of toilet training.

You Might Be A United Methodist If...

you feel a twinge of guilt when you sing "Onward Christian soldiers" with gusto.

You
Might Be A
United
Methodist
If...

you say "trespasses" instead of "debts" or "sins" in the Lord's Prayer but have no idea why.

You Might Be A United Methodist If...

you serve on two or more church committees and are the chairperson of one.

You Might Be A United Methodist If...

you realize that a "chairperson" isn't a furniture maker.

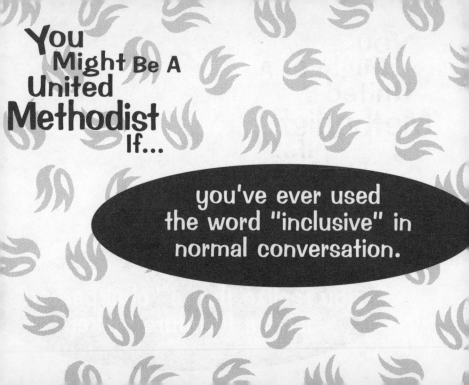

You Might Be A United Methodist If...

the scripture readings during worship come from a "gender neutral" version of the Bible.

You Might Be A United Methodist If...

your Annual Conference spends most of its time debating resolutions that nobody ever reads.

You Might Be A United Methodist If...

you've ever attended an Annual Conference and actually enjoyed it.

You Might Be A United Methodist If...

your congregation uses environmentally friendly paper coffee cups that burn your fingers.

You Might Be A United Methodist If...

you realize a "Cabinet" isn't a storage place for dishes.

You Might Be A United Methodist If...

coffee hour is your favorite part of Sunday morning.

You Might Be A United Methodist If...

you worry that hugging a member of the opposite sex during the passing of the peace might be considered sexual harassment.

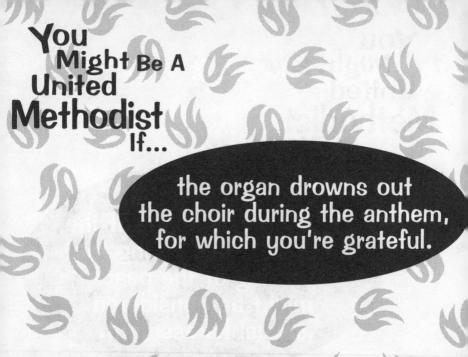

You Might Be A United Methodist If...

your pastor moves every four or five years and you like it that way.

You Might Be A United Methodist If...

"tithing" is encouraged, but widely ignored, during your congregation's annual stewardship campaign.

You Might Be A United Methodist If...

you'd rather be branded with a hot iron than serve on the Nominating Committee.

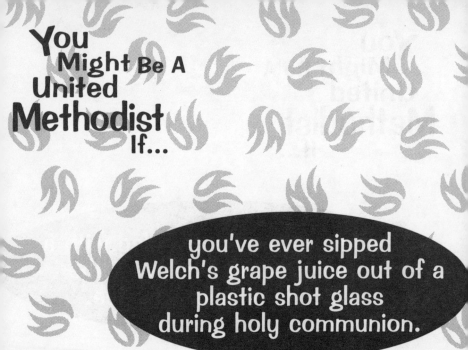

You Might Be A United Methodist If...

you spend more time in church committee meetings than in worship and Sunday school.

You Might Be A United Methodist If...

names like Aldersgate, Asbury, and Epworth are vaguely familiar.

You Might Be A United Methodist If...

you attend the annual "charge conference" only when your pastor engages in power begging.

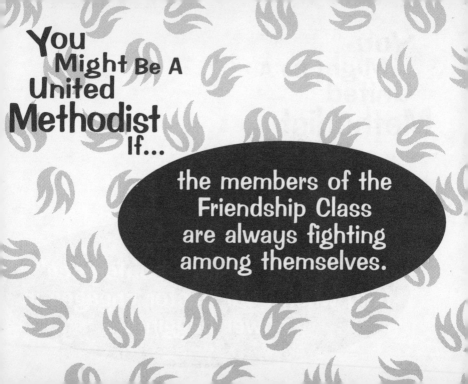

You Might Be A United Methodist If...

you realize that sprinkling, pouring, and immersing are not ways of seasoning food.

You Might Be A United Methodist If...

you're asked to donate money to a "special offering" every other Sunday.

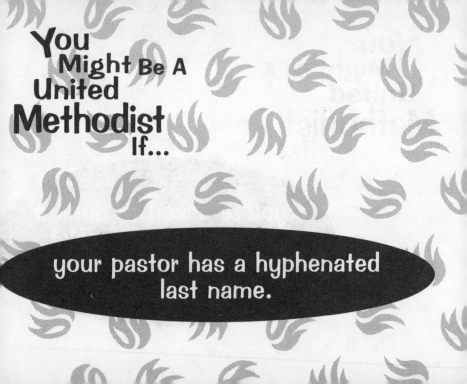

You Might Be A United Methodist If...

you pore over the Conference Journal with the same intensity as you would read a John Grisham novel.

You Might Be A United Methodist If...

you have to fight through a cadre of "designated greeters" to get into the sanctuary.

You Might Be A United Methodist If...

Confirmation Sunday is the last time you see most of the confirmands in church.

You Might Be A United Methodist If...

your pastor responds
to you with,
"I hear you saying..."

You Might Be A United Methodist If...

when the worship service lasts for more than one hour, the beeping of watch alarms drowns out the final hymn.